EDEN *miniatures*

EDEN *miniatures*

Dimensions
Heart
The Snowflake Collector
The Ice King
The Planet Walk
The Tape
Istanbul
Sedartis
Encounters
The Bournemouth & Boscombe Trilogy
Insomnia
Euphoria

EUPHORIA

Optimist

Euphoria

First Edition

Euphoria was first published as part of *EDEN by FREI – a concept narrative in the here & now about the where, the wherefore and forever* at EDENbyFREI.net

{Orlando} was first published as part of *Orlando in the Cities* by Sebastian Michael in *A Quantum City,* Birkhäuser 2015.

ISBN: 978-1-64370-455-5

Optimist Books by Optimist Creations

optimistcreations.com

Euphoria

Experiment

Human Genome, ELISE Phase IV – Interim Summary & Recommendation

The Earth Life Intelligence Study Enterprise continues, with the human genome now entering its fourth significant phase, which it variously labels *The Digital Age, The Information Age,* also just *Digitality,* or any number of variants on these, highlighting, correctly, that it has reached the level at which in similar studies elsewhere life forms have unlocked their next evolutionary plateau by enabling hybrids, augmented organisms and, most importantly, intelligence iterations that are independent of their conduit, consequently relieving them of their evolutionary burden over time.

Phase IV follows Phases I, II and III—the agricultural phase, the enlightenment phase and the industrial phase—which the genome has undergone to varying degrees but which can't, by any means, be considered concluded, either severally or jointly, or let alone—and this applies to any of these phases—in their entirety. Different populations in different geographical areas have attained these at different times in different ways, and across societies many groups are still working their way through what might be considered the basics. Phase IV is thus being entered into on a global scale, but with vastly divergent degrees of deliberate adoption, and by an as yet comparatively small proportion of the human earth population overall.

The *summary findings* so far:

- The human genome now has approximately seven to eight billion live iterations, and, as is to be expected, these vary widely in shape, size, outlook, mental and emotional capacity, and, most striking, cultural context. Apart from their as yet unresolved mortality issue, nothing therefore applies to everyone, but much applies to most, and more applies to more of them than many of them think possible, which in itself is noteworthy, as it is in no small measure symptomatic of their far-reaching reality dysfunction: in their majority, now, individuals seem to consider themselves essentially 'unique' and their own tribes or other social groupings as invariably superior or at the very least preferable to others. In actual fact they are remarkably similar, with pretty much identical basic needs and a commonality factor across the species as high as 99.8%-99.9%.

- Speaking of 'reality': the concept still plays a big part for most humans, albeit also a confusing one. By and large, humans accept as reality what is given, and over time they find it increasingly difficult to detach themselves from whatever that happens to be. For obvious reasons, realities that are experienced in the formative years—which for earth humans tend to be the first dozen to dozen and a half—have a particularly strong hold on humans, and many, quite endearingly, consider whatever they happened to grow up with to be 'normal'.

- This phenomenon notwithstanding, humans are remarkably adaptable, which in large parts accounts for their considerable proliferation. Though at first glance and in the short term they often appear reluctant to embrace the 'other', the 'new', or the 'different', they are absolutely capable of turning a reality set inside out within one generation, and behaviour that one series of fully functioning adults would find completely 'normal'—being whipped to within drawing blood as a child, for example, owning slaves, males marrying several females but stoning to death males who maintain sexual relations with other males—to the next series becomes utterly deplorable, even criminal; while behaviours previously seen as either criminal or at the very least decidedly odd, such as members of the same natural gender cohabiting, getting married and raising offspring, or people eschewing all produce derived from certain other earth species, for example fellow mammals, may, within a generation or two, become entirely acceptable, even celebrated.

- Similarly responsible for their survival thus far is their resilience. Typically, humans can cope with deprivation, hardship and quite unimaginable suffering as long as they consider it unavoidable or deem it imposed on them by a greater and unimpeachable authority, such as a god: they will accept any random calamity or social injustice and virtually any level of pain as long as they can conceptualise it as 'god given' or 'fate', but they will not put up forever with manmade perpetrations of injury.

- Having said that, paradoxical—indeed rationally completely indefensible—thinking and therefore behaviour persists even (sometimes it seems particularly) where it flies in the face of reason or intellectually sound argumentation. Humans can, in the same breath, elevate reason and rational thinking to a paragon, yet remain stubbornly blind to any adjustments to their reality that this by necessity and consequence entails. They may, for example, know—and be in possession of ample data to understand—that the higher a society's levels of incarceration, the higher its reoffending rate, and therefore the higher the social and material cost of failing to integrate or reintegrate members who for whatever reason arrive at the point where they commit crimes against their fellow humans, yet obstinately cling on to barbaric punitive methods that manifestly compound rather than alleviate the cause of their suffering.

- Correspondingly, the genome finds itself in a state of semi-consciousness at which it is aware of its own existence but has no real idea of its meaning or how it fits into any other part of the universe it inhabits, let alone anything beyond that minuscule bubble, of which it has only the faintest of perceptions (and these are vastly distorted). At the same time its fundamental organic needs (the programme, remember, still largely considers itself set to 'survival & propagation', having only in exceptional circumstances advanced significantly beyond its own defaults) are so trivial and basic that by and large and for the body of its own bell curve, it values most things crass and insignificant, while despising anything it feels threatened by as 'too abstract' or 'cultivated'; it delights in cataclysm as much as it fears it, and relishes narratives of destruction, disaster, violence and instability, manufacturing for itself a soup of meaningless noise, while at the same time looking for meaning absolutely everywhere, even where there clearly is none: coincidences, statistical necessities and simple probabilistic patterns are elevated to quasi divine interventions, and by the exact same token, all but the most obvious connections and correlations, especially those not or ill understood by its current (still pretty rudimentary) science it simply ignores or, in some cases vehemently, objects to and refutes.

- Even so, having latched on to information as a thing distinct from energy, and having started to play with quantum phenomena to the point of being able to utilise them, there is hope that the species and therefore the genome will come to recognise the Connexum and begin to view itself in a much larger, much more integrated and also at once much more meaningful and perhaps less significant context than it has hitherto been able to do.

The *interim recommendation* therefore:

The human genome has, in spite of its many obvious (and also many more subtle) failings been spectacularly successful, and although it currently faces some formidable challenges, these are entirely congruent with its level of generative evolution.

This type of evolution, against its own timeframe, is characteristically slow and often marked by greatly frustrating setbacks, which some iterants, especially those who find themselves ahead of the curve or on the crest of the wave, may experience as near-catastrophic regressions.

These are not, however, anything out of the ordinary for a life form such as the one that is here being observed, and having itself now spawned a type of intelligence which is likely to outperform its conduit by exponential orders of magnitude ere long, it stands a good chance of rendering itself obsolete on its own terms in due course, imparting to its generated new genus enough of its own priorities to remain recognisable as a relevant intermediate development stage.

Significantly, this germinating Phase IV holds some considerable promise that either within its own term or during an ensuing fifth or sixth phase, earth intelligence may mature to the point where it can link up with other intelligent entities in its local or any neighbouring cosmic cluster, and so the recommendation therefore is to keep the experiment running, at least for the time being.

Sedartis

{Orlando}

i am orlando

breathless
at the bacchanal
bewitched, senses
submerged, my image
mirrored, my mind
magicked, my emotions
modulated
magnified
unmoderated and maybe
immodest, myself
multiplied:

masked dancer at the carnival
bald bearded lady, fashionista
beehive diva, torch song bearer of my soul

pole-dancing scientist
shop floor assistant checking out
the other side, experimenter, part-time
   genius
moustachioed hipster sophist nerd geek
   self-inventor and
bespectacled spectator
taking in, in-
haling, hailing without praise or
condemnation
participant observer, being-done-to
doer

all exposed

the pushing
to the fore, persistent rushing shoreward
   of
wave upon wave:
the daily deluge of disaster
wilfully

constructed, or else
wantonly permitted to occur and then
dispersed
with breathless kick and fury
horned-up with excitement
round the clock
catastrophe porn paired with power
   penetration to the
brain: every
second someone selling something
a tsunami of musthave dispensables
then news again the weather breaking
   down ten thousand perish in a flood
security alert
three men arrested at the airport
one who fled
soft-spoken leaker of state secrets swears
   allegiance to
the people; people
protest
the police, the army

bullets rifles hand grenades, ex-
superpower eyeing up her neighbours'
  territories, boundaries
unkept, unrecognised, rendered irrelevant
space probe touchdown on the comet,
  cheers and champagne at
base, break through
the tunnel, high speed trains
dark matter and dark energy
the murder of the messengers
a million on the streets in solidarity,
  fighters
of and for freedom feeling pain, offenders
in each other's eyes – our
tears taste all the same

a smartphone
with an app the university that taps into
  the global lecture hall
a telescope array across a mountain table
  peering deep into the origin of

time, and
cupcakes
talent shows, made-up
realities
downloads, stolen
identities and
printed body parts
milestones in mending memories, the
tantalising likelihood that we are not
  alone
sandcastles made of stars, stars
made of frivolities
cat videos
and piles
and piles
of rubbish

rejects
refugees
residents of uncertainty, nomads by
adverse conditions, the

collateral of calamity
unwanted
unloved, un-
understood
disowned dishonoured dismissed
   dishevelled, dis-
affected
indistinct
in the morass
of mass
morbidity, in-
visible

flashes of inspiration
fascinations
colours, glitter
decadences
balls: exuberances
festivals and
congregations, close
communions

travel at the speed of sound, lightspeed
communication
instantaneous pools of
commonality
the vibe and exultation, the
euphoria
the sharpwit razor of precision, the
ingeniousness
the shared experience
the climactic joy, the
sacred orgasm of
life

i rest
i pause
i meditate, i am
orlando
i reflect

i have no solution, there are no solutions
i have no anger: anger is void, i
ease
i learn
i think
i offer

silence

i
become
the citizen
and i see sparks of wisdom and then once
again i laugh
i love
i give
i take
i lose myself
i win

i love again, i want and want not and
want not to want, i
realise
i am a part of it: i am
a part
of everything, every
thing
is part of me

i am the gods
i am the universe
i am the energy
i am the code
i am the probability
i am the failure and the hope and the
despair
i am the triumph
of existence

that is what i am:

i
am

orlando

Expiration

We are not doomed.

We may well be determined and we may be defined but we are not definitive and we won't go on forever and we won't ever die: immortality is granted, though the wish is monstrous, as long as we take it upon ourselves to be the centre of our own attention.

Conduits to the stream. The energy, the code, the connection. We may yet go extinct; we need not mourn ourselves: we leave behind perhaps no legacy but our intention to do well.

Complex situations, simple choices: do you put anger in the world and hatred and want and division and them versus us and incomprehension and rejection, hostility, enmity, loss; or do you put hope. Do you put recognition, respect. Enjoinment: empathy. Different, differentiated manifestations of one and the same.

Never even mind that we're human: remember we are god. When every mistake we've ever made is multiplied with every catastrophe, our hearts may hurt from the unwisdom we yield to. And yet: we can make it so, we can make it other.

The thing that we're made of may yet lift us. We can, whether we want to or not; but wanting to is harder than saying no.

Everything is known, everyone can be understood.

Accept as the deepest part of you that which you loathe most. The person you despise: you are him, you are her. Embrace them. The child murderess. The suicide bomber. The bludgeoner to death. You celebrate, you cheer, you dance your pride when your football team wins. When your psychopath strikes: suffer him to be your disaster no less than you appropriate your goal scorer's triumph. The medals on the athlete's chest are badges of your honour no more and no less than the bloodstains on the knife stabber's hand are witness to your failure. Own it.

Grow up into the painful truths, and free yourself. There is no freedom without truth. There is no truth without pain.

There is no pain that does not carry a reward. When all is said and done: start over. There is no reward without loss. There is no loss without self. There is no self that stands alone.

Surrender to the motion of a greater purpose. Even if you don't understand. Even if you do not believe. Even if you're not convinced. Your heart knows long before your brain, because your brain is more powerful than you think: when knowledge is you and you are the world and the world is an instance in just one universe and the universe is a thought and the thought is expressed then you are god: you are god.

Accept the burden of being all powerful. Make good on your promise. Dare love.

{Vernation}

i am
these days it appears
attractive to young men
attracted too, of course, but that's not
   news
and not newsworthy: young men are
attractive
by definition
even people who aren't generally attracted
   to young men can see this
and even if they can't see it, they are still
attracted to them
irrespective
their gender their inclination their
orientation
their emotion their wisdom their
   inhibition, their assessment of any given

situation:
whether they want to or not and believe
  that they are or that they aren't
people
all people
are
always
attracted to
young men
(except those few who are not and they
  are few and are not and are therefore the
exception.)
the rule
is confirmed
what's new is that more than before
more than ever
as far as i ever can tell
(and often i can't)
or recall (and i could if i would)
men half my age or just slightly older or
  occasionally just slightly younger still too

come to me, seek me out
not i them
of the men i have met, spoken to, spent
time and been with lately
most, though not all, have been those
that are half my age or slightly older or on
occasion slightly younger even
and who have come to me, sought me out
not i them
this flatters me, of course, maybe honours
me, but more than that does it
fascinate me
because i don't do anything to attract
them, not
consciously: if anything i do the opposite
i grow a beard
i wear a jacket left me by a friend
more than ten years ago, which was
vintage then
my shoes are worn out and my jeans
though skinny

threadbare
i don't go to the gym i don't wear my
lenses i don't
cultivate
a young voice or vocabulary
yet
young men
more than they have ever done before,
even when
especially
when i was their age
come to me, seek me out
i don't go after them. on a park bench at a
party in a bar
even online
i mind my own business more or less
i say hello maybe, or
greet a smile with a smile
but that's it
i don't do anything more; maybe
that's what it is

maybe that's what makes me
suddenly, perplexingly
attractive
to young men: it may be that
in the past, when i was
their age
i was just trying too hard to be
something, someone, some other
person than the one that they saw
because they saw through me then to me
  now
and now
what they see is what they get
and if they are friendly and kind and
  intelligent too
(apart from being attractive: being young,
  they're always
obviously
attractive)
i see no reason
why they shouldn't get

what they see if
what they see is
what they desire
is life not give and take after all and are we
  not in it
to share of ourselves
as we lose ourselves in each other?

my summer of love leaves me warm-hearted
  light-headed and simple of soul
there is
so much
delight
in being
human

Obsolemnum

Then always the inherent question to self: am I going to be one who says, I would if I could, or am I going to be one who says, I could and I did. It's a loaded question, heavy with expectation, anxiety; pressure, even. And it's also maybe the wrong question. Because if I could and I did, what is remarkable about that? Isn't that what we do: what we can? If we don't do what we can, then what do we do?

So is the more pertinent question: am I going to be one who says, I could and I did, or am I going to be one who says, I couldn't but I did all the same: I found a way. I learnt how to do it. I overcame my reluctance, my objections, my fear. I surmounted the obstacles, of which there were many. I was told what I wanted to do was impossible and I said: I hear you. I don't believe you. I believe what I have in mind may be difficult, it may be near unattainable, but impossible is nothing. I shall do it anyway. And if that is my way, and my way alone.

There are so many who opine. There are so many voices that make up the din of the world. There are so many who have tried, and tell you so. There are so many who know how it's done. From experience, from having done it themselves. There are so many who will dispense with advice, with counsel, with rules. These rules that are being laid down by being followed. These patterns we draw on the mindscape of our culture by walking the path that has already been walked, often enough for it to be seen, to be recognised, to be followed, again, and again; to be treaded into the ground, until it appears inescapable: that's the way, the only way to go. No other way seems possible now, it has been decreed. Not by authority, maybe, by convention.

What if the question is this: am I going to be one who says, I took the path of least resistance, the path that was already mapped out for me, the path that I could follow, conveniently, because it had been taken many times before—so much so, it had become a road, and one much travelled—or am I going to be one who says: I saw the path, I recognised it, of course. It held no appeal to me. I was curious to know. What lies beyond the path. Where does the non-road lead. Whom shall I meet, and what encounter, if I take the unmarked route. So that's what I did. I got stuck, many times, I took turns that weren't so much wrong as simply dead ends. I had to double back on myself on occasion, and I cut myself in the thicket. My feet hurt, and my head. My limbs were weary with travel, with toil. I was alone, sometimes lonely. There were nights when I cried for want of shelter, for want of care, for want of some body to hold on to, for some mind to reassure me, for some light to guide me. I persevered, I continued. I had to. It was either that or the abandonment of myself: failure complete. It was either going on, or getting lost entirely, in the wilderness. It was either holding on to the hope, the idea, to the notion that there is something yet to be discovered, something yet to be said, something yet to be thought that is in one sense or other worthwhile, that has not, in every possible manner, been expressed before, that is not fully known, or becoming obsolete.

Am I going to be one who says, I tried, I wish sometimes I'd tried harder, but at least I tried. Or am I going to be one who says, I tried and tried again and I did not give up and whatever the outcome—is there an outcome, ever? and is that the point? or is the point not a point but a wave and that wave is the process, the doing, the thinking, the loving, the giving, the taking, the seeing, the learning, the sending, the receiving, the being?—I put my all into it. Am I going to be one who says, things happened to me and I made it through, or am I going to be one who says, I am the things that I did.

Yet to what end? There is no end. Then to what purpose? Let the purpose be bigger than me, greater, if I dare think it so: nobler. Let the purpose be the ideal, the aspiration. Not for myself, but for my world. The world not as it is now, the world as I know it could be. That 'better world' that is forever in our power to create and seems forever out of reach. Because it is, both. But what if that is meaningless, what if we all mean nothing at all and are simple quirks of short-lived accidental matter in a constellation of incomprehensible—because random—energy fluctuations that have no purpose, that have no meaning, that have no end and no beginning, that may or may as well not exist?

What does that concern me now? Who cares if it matters or not? What need do

I have for a reason? What I know is I am
here, and I have so much time, maybe less,
perhaps a bit more.

What matters then, surely, is only that
I be, in the end, one who says, that was
my time well spent, that was my cards—
whatever these cards were—well played;
that was my fellow humans loved, my
world respected; that was my work well
done, my life well lived.

{Palimpsest}

What, then, if it is true.

What, then, if it is true that we live in this world.

What then, if it is true that we live in this world and this world is the best of all possible worlds.

What then, if it is true that we live in this world and this world is the best of all possible worlds but not the only possible world merely the best of all possible worlds right now made by us for us because every possible world is the best of all possible worlds at that moment in that place in that configuration; there are an infinite number of infinities so there must be an infinite number of dimensions and an infinite number of potentialities.

What then if we were all of them at any given time.

What then if we were to learn to experience life like that.

What then if we were to learn to experience life like that and sense that we are everything we can imagine to be and everything we can't imagine to be and that therefore everything is exactly as it should be if we will it so.

What though if we were to fail ourselves in our entirety and simply not realise our potential.

What though if we were to fail ourselves in our entirety and simply not realise our potential.

What though if we were to fail ourselves in our entirety and simply not realise our potential but know that that's what we were doing and know that doing this was unnecessary:

What then if we were to know that we are able to realise our potential —

What then if we were to know that we are able to realise our potential, at least part of our potential —

What then if we were to realise at least more of the potentiality than hitherto we had known about —

What if we were to know this and act upon it; what if we were to know this and act upon it, then what would we do? What if we were to know this and act upon it: then what would we do?

What, then, if we were to know that we can realise our potential, and act upon it.

What would we do.

(I ache for my mind to expand. Not expand just a little to know a thing or two more, I ache for my mind to expand to the dimensions it can not yet comprehend through the layers it can not yet penetrate, beyond the colours on the spectrum to the prisms the frequencies to the scales it isn't capable yet of taking in. I long, I long for it to make sense, in a way:

a different kind of sense, a sense that I had
never known could be made.

I yearn to absorb and be
absorbed.
I long, I
long
to)

exist

Euphoria

I look at myself. Not in the mirror, not as a person with a yen for profundity and meaning, but in a picture. I find the picture among my belongings as I clear out my flat because it's being renovated: for the first time in decades I go through every object I own and therefore am owned by and decide whether to keep it, or whether to part. Keep it or part. Keep? Or part: divest, my mind mostly suggests, and my heart, in most cases, though not quite all, affirms, yes divest!

I am unambitious but consistent in the pursuit of my task, as I progress through each item one by one. I look at every photograph, and every photograph looks at me. I don't notice me at first, not in an 'oh, here I am, look at me!' kind of way. I just know I'm there. In the picture. As anyone ever photographed by necessity is. In this particular stack, I am part of a collection of early black and white ten by eights that I must have had done when I first decided to be an actor. This dates them in the mid to late nineteen-eighties and me at about twenty-two, twenty-three. I don't notice me, not this time round. I'm simply there.

The second time round I notice myself. I have been away for seven weeks, nearly eight, and I've come back into my flat, which is all new and fresh and still so familiar and more home now than ever, and as I unpack the boxes I once again go through almost every thing I own and am therefore owned by, only this time I do so not one by one but in batches, just to make sure. And this time round I jump out at myself: I am beautiful. I wish I'd known that. I wish I'd known then that I was beautiful, but I didn't. I still don't. But I was. And I am. Only I can't feel it now, I can't even see it. I couldn't then. But I can now see it then. I can now see that then I am beautiful. I have a gentle face and searching eyes, and an almost translucent skin; I have my life in front of me; not my childhood, not my youth, but my whole adult existence.

I am overcome with compassion. How brave I was, and needed to be. How unencumbered I was. How I looked forward, unafraid. How strong. How fragile. How soft, how resilient; how steadfast. How honest. How vulnerable. How resolute not to hurt, not to fail, or if to hurt then not to cry, not to grumble, and not to succumb; yet to prevail...

I sense the time has come. I trust it now, much more, the sense. All the things I know and all the things I don't know are the same: they all abide by and reside in me. No words of wisdom, no advice. Let me make my own mistakes. Let sorrow, loss and lingering despair crush me to tears. I won't protect me from myself: that would be crueller still.

Across from me, at the Limonlu Bahçe, Istanbul: George. I lean forward a little, my chair creaks, he looks up at me, curious, askance. Unimpressed. Unruffled. Unspoilt. Unused. Undamaged. Unfathomable, even to me. I know how you feel, I've been there, believe me, I've been you, but no, I don't know you at all.

I know you no more than I know any boy your age. Man! You never liked being a boy much, a youth, maybe, yes; do you like being a man? I hear myself think the question, and in a flicker of recognition—probably imagined, only by me—he says: 'Do you relish being a man?' ('Relish.' That's better. 'Like' is so lightweight, it's neither here nor there. He could have said 'enjoy' but that, too, has long since been eroded, diminished to some middling marketed meaninglessness.)

'I do.' I say: 'I will. If I haven't till now, then henceforth I shall.'

'Henceforth?' He gives me that smile, that bemused, too knowing, wry play on his lips, a light in his eye.

I don't want to burden myself with the responsibility of having interfered with my own life. Not here, not now. I used to be troubled. Then charming. Then enigmatic. I'm still working on wise.

'Be generous, be kind.' (I thought I was not going to give me advice. Is it that hard to refrain?) 'Forgive. Live and let live, and trust the universe is on your side.' He looks at me, unsmiling, unconcerned, frank. He knows all this already, everyone does. 'Felicity, fortune and favour all balance out, over time. Take your time. Let not there ever be any hurry. Go you about with a heart that beats warm and a mind that keeps open and a soul that is free, and your path will lead you where you need to be.' (That's done it: I've lost him.) His eyes linger long and soft, not hard; then, inscrutable now, he nods. 'Just remember...' (Stop it! *Stop it now!* No counsel, no words, no well-intentioned guidance from yonder!) '...if you want a squirt of milk in your pail you have to squeeze the odd teat now and then.'

I get up; the temptation to ruffle his hair proves almost too much, but I know I used to hate this, and so I desist.

'Fare well.' I say, in two words. He looks up at me and, unsmiling still, but gamely returns: 'Fare thee well.'

And then I remember and I turn around to him before I leave and I stand at the bottom of the steps that lead up through the house, from the garden, onto the street, and the garden is busy again now, and buzzing, and I see myself sitting there, alone but not lonely, quiet, composed, a little aloof, just the way I was in that photograph, just the way I now feel, and I spread my arms to this Garden of Eden afore me and I demand, at the top of my voice, of it all: '*BE MAGNIFICENT!*'

And, having said what I needed to say now, I leave myself to my self: my adventure, my journey, my love.

And here I was and I will be, but mostly now, here I am.

(The good thing about fiction? I unimagine it, and it's gone...)

www.ingramcontent.com/pod-product-compliance
Ingram Content Group UK Ltd.
Pitfield, Milton Keynes, MK11 3LW, UK
UKHW041842200726
13854UKWH00005BA/199
9 781643 704555